University of Toronto

The Benefactors of the University of Toronto

After the Great Fire of 14th February, 1890

University of Toronto

The Benefactors of the University of Toronto
After the Great Fire of 14th February, 1890

ISBN/EAN: 9783337035334

Printed in Europe, USA, Canada, Australia, Japan

Cover: Foto ©ninafisch / pixelio.de

More available books at **www.hansebooks.com**

University of Toronto.

THE

BENEFACTORS

OF THE

UNIVERSITY OF TORONTO,

After the Great Fire of 14th February, 1890.

PUBLISHED FOR THE UNIVERSITY OF TORONTO

BY

THE WILLIAMSON BOOK CO., TORONTO.

1892.

TO

Her Majesty, the Queen, Empress of India,

HIS MAJESTY, THE GERMAN EMPEROR,

HIS MAJESTY, THE KING OF SAXONY,

HIS MAJESTY, THE KING OF WÜRTTEMBERG,

HIS ROYAL HIGHNESS THE PRINCE OF WALES,

AND TO ALL THEIR GENEROUS BENEFACTORS,

THE SENATE AND COUNCIL OF THE UNIVERSITY,

THE COUNCIL OF UNIVERSITY COLLEGE,

AND THE

BOARD OF TRUSTEES,

UNITE IN TENDERING GRATEFUL THANKS FOR KIND SYMPATHY AND
LIBERAL, PRACTICAL AID IN THEIR TIME OF NEED.

President.

BY a disastrous fire on the evening of the 14th of February, 1890, the main building of the University of Toronto, including the Convocation Hall, Museums and Library, was reduced to a roofless and defaced ruin. In accordance with a practice of long standing, the building had been given up to the use of the undergraduates for their Annual Conversazione. Among the scientific attractions prepared for the occasion, the programme announced a display of bacteriological and other microscopic slides. Some of the lamps provided for the illumination of the microscopes were upset. As the furnaces and radiators, required for the heating of the building, had been in constant use for upwards of four months, the whole woodwork was so thoroughly dry, that on the flame catching the flooring, saturated with the spilt oil, it spread with such rapidity that the main portion of the building was speedily enveloped in flames. The conflagration involved the loss of the entire contents of the Library, along with a considerable portion of the valuable collections in the Biological and Ethnological Museums, and the whole of those in the departments of Mineralogy and Geology.

The library, though only formed in recent years, had been selected with great care, under the advice of the heads of the various departments in the University; and already contained a selection of upwards of 33,000 volumes, including rare and valuable works, along with complete sets of scientific and literary serials, of importance as books of reference alike for professors and students.

The University building was regarded with just pride by the graduates as admittedly the most beautiful structure devoted to academic purposes on the American continent; and, as one of the chief ornaments of the city of Toronto, its loss was deplored by many besides those who associated its architectural features with the cherished memories of their *Alma Mater*. Happily, the structure proved to be so substantial that the walls admitted of restoration and re-roofing; though much of the fine carving had been defaced, or had scaled off under the intense heat of the conflagration. Externally, the University Building has now been restored to more than its original beauty: advantage having been taken of the opportunity, to remove some objectionable features that detracted from its symmetry as a whole. It is scarcely possible to overestimate the æsthetic influences of noble architecture in a building so intimately associated with the intellectual training of the rising generation at the most impressible period of life. But the value of this is exceptionally great in a young country, and on a new continent, where no monuments of ancient or mediæval art are to be seen, such as are familiar to the undergraduate in the seats of learning of the mother-land. The influences springing from such a source play their part in the cultured refinement which is not the least valuable element of higher education; and constitute an important factor in the enduring associations which link the graduate to his *alma mater*.

Through the liberality of the Provincial Legislature, supplemented by a generous gift from that of Quebec, and by the prompt and kindly aid of private benefactors, the restoration of the main structure has been prosecuted with so little delay, that, though still incomplete, the authorities were able to resume University work in the restored building in October, 1891; and on re-assembling after the Christmas holidays, in January, 1892, they entered on its full occupation, with greatly enlarged accommodation. It is now provided with many novel facilities suggested by experience, or derived from the most modern examples of improved lecture-rooms, laboratories, museums, and other appliances in the Universities of Great Britain, France, and Germany, and in those of the United States. The old Convocation Hall having been found inadequate for the requirements of the University, it is purposed, as soon as funds are available, to erect a new one in near proximity to the main building, on a scale adapted to the great increase in the number of undergraduates, and to the special uses for which experience has shown it to be applicable. The Biological Museum has been provided with adequate space in the new science buildings; and plans are now approved of for a building to be immediately proceeded with, which will furnish to the department of Chemistry greatly extended facilities, with the requisite laboratories and lecture-rooms. The departments of Geology and Mineralogy must in like manner be provided for by further extension of the science buildings; and ample provision for the accommodation of the

Library will be secured in the new structure now erecting on the east side of the College lawn. The changes thus projected and already in progress, whereby the Convocation Hall, Library and Museums are transferred to other sites, have placed a large amount of space in the restored building at the disposal of the Faculties for additional laboratories, lecture-rooms, and other requirements of great value in the daily work of instruction and research.

Among the many losses involved in the destruction of the University building, none excited keener feelings of regret than that of the library, and its prized contents. It was a beautiful hall, fitted up with carved oaken alcoves and galleries, after the model of the older university libraries of Europe. The vista was terminated by a fine statue of William of Wykeham, originally executed by Thomas, the eminent English sculptor, under the direction of Pugin, as an essay-piece for the sculptured decorations of the new parliament buildings at Westminster; and was presented to the University by the Rev. Arthur Wickson, M.A., LL.D., a graduate of the university; and the first to fill the office of classical tutor, under the late

president, the Rev. Dr. McCaul. As the statue of
the founder of New College, Oxford, and the liberal
patron of learning in the age of Chaucer, this fine
work of art was prized as an appropriate adorn-
ment to the Provincial University; and its loss
ranks among the irreparable sacrifices involved in
the fire. But in no department has the wide-felt
sympathy manifested itself with more practical
liberality, as shown in the valuable contributions
to replace the contents of the old library alcoves.
Encouraged by such prompt and efficient aid, no
time has been lost in taking the needful steps for
providing a suitable home for the restored library.
The new structure now in progress on a site
selected for it midway between the buildings appropriated to literary and scientific instruction,
will form an attractive addition to the group of
buildings surrounding the College lawn. The
plans have been carefully prepared with a view
to the construction of a detached, and, as far as
possible, a fire-proof building, embodying the fruits
of the most recent experience both in Europe and
in the United States. The book room, adapted
for the secure accommodation of the entire collection within narrow limits, has been planned on a

scale to admit of the reception of 120,000 volumes, with provision for future extension. To this a set of seminary rooms, or studies, will be attached appropriated to the leading departments of science, letters, and philosophy. It is further proposed that the entire building shall be illuminated with the electric light, and so furnish an attractive resort where the student may pass his evenings with no less pleasure than profit. With the improvements thus aimed at, it is confidently anticipated that the new library will prove an invaluable adjunct to the scheme of higher education embraced in the special organization of the University of Toronto, as a common centre of intellectual life ; and will constitute a bond of closer union among the Federating Colleges of the Provincial University.

It may be permissible, without detracting from the assurance of heartfelt gratitude extended to all the benefactors hereafter named, to single out from among the prized contributions to the Library, now amounting to 40,970 volumes, a few that possess special value, by reason of some exceptional characteristic. But the first acknowledgments are due to those spontaneous organizations

of sympathising friends, both in England and on
the Continent, to whose effective labours such
practical results are largely to be ascribed. To the
English Committee, presided over by the Marquis
of Lorne, embracing in its members men of the
highest eminence in rank, in science, and letters,
with the efficient services of Alexander Staveley
Hill, Esq., Q.C., M.P., as its treasurer, and Sir George
Baden-Powell, M.P., as its secretary : the University
has been placed under lasting obligations for contributions of choice works in all departments of
science and literature. The presentation plates on
many of the volumes in the restored Library will
perpetuate the recognition of the services thus
rendered in the time of need by this influential
English Committee; and will preserve for later
generations a record of this practical evidence of
the ties of kinship and common nationality that
bind us to the mother-land ; while they will con-
cur with us in welcoming no less gratefully in
others of the presentation plates evidence of a recognition of the common brotherhood of letters
and science, shown by the Committee organized
in Germany, and by the Faculties of sister universities both in the Old and the New World.

To the Marquis of Lorne, and the English "University Library Restoration Committee," the authorities of the University of Toronto tender their sincere acknowledgments for the unwearied labour expended on their behalf, and for the prized contributions which constitute such effective help in replacing one of their greatest losses.

To Dr. John Landauer, of Brunswick, and the Committee of eminent German scholars and patrons of letters, who have co-operated in securing valued gifts from distinguished foreign authors, from publishers, and other liberal sympathisers, the authorities of the University record their hearty thanks; with the assurance of their high estimation of the services thus rendered to them.

To all the many liberal donors, Foreign and Colonial Governments, Learned Societies, Authors, Publishers, and private Benefactors: the Chancellor, Vice-Chancellor, and President of the University, the Senate, University Council, and Faculties, unite in the presentation of grateful acknowledgments for practical manifestations of liberal sympathy; which, with the additions since made by purchase, will enable them to enter on the occupation of their new library—as they confidently hope, at the beginning of the new Academic year in October next,—with a collection of between forty and fifty thousand volumes.

Without attempting to discriminate among the many benefactors, whose names and gifts are enumerated below, it will not be unacceptable to the friends of the University to be presented with a brief résumé indicative of the wide and varied character of the sympathy awakened on behalf of the University of Toronto, when the knowledge of its losses became known; and foremost in the record of prized donations must be ranked the costly and beautifully bound works, the gift of Her Majesty the Queen, which it is to be fondly hoped will survive to be the pride of many generations of graduates, perpetuating the loved and revered name of Victoria on our roll of benefactors.*

Gifts, including works from their own pens, as well as other valuable additions to the

---

* As this acknowledgment of the generous liberality of many benefactors is passing through the press, the announcement has been received of a valuable gift, about to be forwarded to the University Library, comprising nearly five hundred volumes, which have been selected under the orders of His Majesty, the German Emperor, from the duplicates of the Libraries of Berlin, Breslau, Königsberg, Bonn, Göttingen, Greifswalde, Halle, Münster, Braunsberg and Erfurt. The gratifying announcement also reaches us that their Majesties the Kings of Saxony and Württemberg have been pleased to grant donations to the Library.

library, have been received from His Royal Highness the Prince of Wales, the Prince of Monaco, the
late Duke of Devonshire, the Duke of Argyle, the
Marquis of Ripon, the Marquis of Lorne, the Earl
of Rosebery, the Earl of Selborne, the Dowager
Lady Vernon, and other noble donors. The names
of Universities, Academies, and learned Societies
of Europe, Asia, and America, the contributors of
valuable gifts of their transactions, proceedings,
and other publications, are recorded with grateful
pride in our list of benefactors. Among those, the
costly liberality of Oxford comprises a selection of
choice volumes to the value of £500 sterling, from
the publications of the Clarendon press, every one
of them a welcome contribution to our shelves.
Cambridge sends its gift of like character, including
the entire publications of the Pitt press. From the
Universities of Edinburgh and Aberdeen and from
Trinity College, Dublin; from the Universities of
Christiania, Copenhagen, Marburg, Strassburg, and
Upsala; from Harvard, Columbia College, Prince-
ton, Cornell, Michigan, Amherst, Johns Hopkins,
Kansas, and other American universities; from the
University of Melbourne, and from our own Cana-
dian Universities and Colleges, as well as personally

from members of their Faculties, many valued contributions are gratefully acknowledged.

Not only to the British Government, but to the Governments of France, Germany, Sweden, Spain, Italy, Switzerland, and the United States, we have to render no less grateful thanks for aid in restoring to the University the indispensable appliances of a well-furnished library.

From his Excellency the Governor-General of India, personally, as well as from the Secretary of State for India; from Australia; from the colonies of Victoria and New South Wales; and from the Asiatic Society of Tokyo, Japan, contributions have reached us, accompanied with greetings of kindly sympathy that give an additional value to such practical manifestations of good will. One of the latest of such welcome greetings comes from Victoria, a sister colony at the Antipodes, stating that the gift is sent as "a mark of sympathy with the University in its recent troubles; of respect for the high courage with which they were met; and in token of a warm desire for closer relations between two great colonies of the British Empire."

To the disinterested liberality of many of the leading publishing houses of England, France, Germany, Italy, and the United States, acknowledgments are no less heartily due for valuable contributions of books.

But one class of acquisitions may, without invidious distinction, be selected for special note, while gratefully returning thanks to all our benefactors. The works presented to us under such circumstances, connecting the authors' names with their gifts, will constitute a feature in the new University Library that cannot fail to possess a peculiar charm 'for all who enjoy the privilege of their use. They include complete sets of the works of the Poet Laureate, Alfred, Lord Tennyson, and of the late Cardinal Manning; and selections from those of Professor Jowett, Sir William Dawson, Professor J. S. Blackie, Professors Lepsius, Mommsen, Brinton, Dr. Francis Parkman, Professor Piazzi Smith, Sir Lyon Playfair, President G. Stanley Hall, Dr. G. Humphrey, Dr. G. Birkbeck Hill, Mr. James Sime, and others, whose names are set forth in the accompanying record. With those, another class of contributions claims a place. For we must rank with authors' gifts, others received from the representatives of those who still live in their works, and " rule our spirits from their urns;" and foremost

B

among such are the volumes presented by Mr Robert Barrett Browning, the son of England's great poet so recently laid to rest in Westminster Abbey, and of England's gifted poetess who lies apart under the cypresses in the city of Dante. With such also may fitly be classed the scientific works of the late Professor Clark Maxwell, forwarded for the Library by the Clark Maxwell Memorial Committee; and along with those may no less appropriately rank, as memorials of another eminent man of science, the gift from the Chatsworth Library of valuable scientific serials bearing the autograph impress of the great English Chemist, the Hon. Henry Cavendish.

A few private gifts have an interest of another kind from their associations with former owners : among which may be specially noted some folios of early date from the library of the Historian of " The Decline and Fall of the Roman Empire "; and other works from those of Edmund Burke and M. Guizot.

One other gift, of unique historical value, is a contemporary MS. report of the trial of the seven Bishops, with the autograph notes of the Solicitor-General, Sir William Williams, who, with Attorney-General Powis, conducted the prosecution.

LIST OF DONORS.

Her Majesty the Queen.
His Majesty the German Emperor.
His Majesty the King of Saxony.
His Majesty the King of Württemberg.
His Royal Highness the Prince of Wales.

Governments and Municipalities.

Arkansas, Superintendent of Public Instruction.
Boston, Board of Health.
Bremen, Bureau für Bremische Statistik.
British Columbia, Provincial Secretary's Dept.
Canada, Customs Department.
Canada, Department of Agriculture, Archives Branch.
Canada, Department of the Interior, Geological and Natura
    History Survey.
Canada, Department of Public Printing.
Canada, Department of Railways and Canals.
Canada, Department of the Secretary of State.
Canada, House of Commons, Distribution Office.
Canada, Library of Parliament.
France, Ministère des Affaires Etrangères.
France, Ministère de l'Agriculture.
France, Ministère du Commerce, de l'Industrie et des Colonies.
France, Ministère de l'Instruction Publique et des Beaux Arts.
France, Ministère de l'Intérieur.
France, Ministère des Travaux Publics.
Geneva, Chancellerie d'État.
Germany, Reichs-Marine-Amt.
Great Britain, Admiralty.

Great Britain, Colonial Office.
Great Britain, Foreign Office.
Great Britain, India Office.
Great Britain, Meteorological Office.
Great Britain, Stationery Office.
Great Britain, Treasury.
Illinois, State Board of Health.
Illinois, State Laboratory of Natural History
Iowa, Superintendent of Public Instruction.
Italy, Ministero degli Affari Esteri.
Italy, Ministero d'Agricoltura, Industria e Commercio.
Italy, Ministero dei Lavori Pubblici.
Italy, Ministero del Tesoro.
Italy, Ufficio Geologico.
Italy, Ministero della Marina
Italy, Direttore della Statistica.
Manitoba, Provincial Secretary's Department.
Massachusetts, State Board of Health.
Michigan, Executive Office.
Michigan, State Board of Health.
Minnesota, Department of State.
Minnesota, Commissioner of Labor.
Minnesota, Geological & Natural History Survey.
Missouri, Superintendent of Public Instruction.
New Brunswick, Provincial Secretary's Department.
New Hampshire, Secretary of State.
New Hampshire, Superintendent of Public Instruction.
New South Wales, Department of Mines.
New York, Board of Health.
New York, State Library.
New York, State Museum.
New York City, Health Department.
Norway, North-Atlantic Expedition, 1876-78.
Nova Scotia, Provincial Secretary's Department.
Ohio, State Forestry Bureau.
Ontario, Department of Agriculture.
Ontario, Legislative Library.

Ontario, Provincial Secretary's Department.
Pennsylvania, State Library.
Prince Edward Island, Provincial Secretary's Department.
Quebec, Provincial Secretary's Department.
Quebec, Legislative Library.
Rhode Island, State Board of Health.
Switzerland, Commission Géologique Suisse.
Switzerland, Commission Géodesique Suisse.
U.S., Dept. of Agriculture, Division of Chemistry.
U.S., Dept. of Agriculture, Division of Entomology. '
U.S., Dept. of Agriculture, Forestry Division.
U.S., Dept. of Agriculture, Secretary's Office.
U.S., Coast and Geodetic Survey.
U.S , Commission of Fish and Fisheries.
U.S., Dept. of the Interior, Bureau of Education.
U.S., Dept. of the Interior, Census Commissioner.
U.S., Dept. of the Interior, Geological Survey.
U.S., Dept. of the Interior, Secretary's office.
U.S., Navy Dept., Bureau of Steam Engineering.
U.S., Navy Department, Naval Observatory.
U.S., Smithsonian Institution.
U.S., Department of State, Bureau of Statistics.
U.S., Treasury Dept., Comptroller of the Currency.
U.S., Treasury Department, Secretary's office.
U.S., War Department, Office of the Chief of Engineers
U.S., War Department, Signal Office.
U.S., War Department, Surgeon-General's office.
U.S., Distribution Office.
Victoria, Government of the Colony of.

Universities and Colleges.

Aberdeen, University of.
Amherst College.
Berlin, Technische Hochschule.
Blankenberg Gymnasium.
Bonn, Rheinische Friedrich-Wilhelms-Universität.

Bowdoin College, Brunswick, U.S.
Bristol, University College.
Cambridge, University of.
Cambridge, Christ's College.
Cambridge, King's College.
Cambridge, Museum of Comparative Zoology.
Cassel, Realschule.
Christiania, Kongelige norske Fredriks Universitet.
Clark University, Worcester, U.S.
Columbia College, New York.
Copenhagen, Universitet.
Cornell University, Ithaca.
Darmstadt, Technische Hochschule.
Dublin, Trinity College.
Edinburgh, University of.
Erlangen, Friedrich-Alexanders-Universität.
Hanover, Technische Hochschule,
Harvard College, Cambridge, U.S.
Howard University, Washington.
Johns Hopkins University, Baltimore.
Laval, Université, Quebec.
Lille, Université de.
London, University College.
Marburg, Universität.
Melbourne, University of.
Michigan, University of, Ann Arbor.
Montpellier, Université de.
Münster, Königliche Akademie.
New Jersey, College of, Princeton.
Oxford, University of.
Panjab University, Lahore.
Perugia, Università.
Queen's University, Kingston.
Royal College of Physicians, London.
Royal College of Surgeons, London.
School of Practical Science, Toronto.
Strassburg, Kaiser-Wilhelms-Universität.

St. Thomas's Hospital Medical School, London.
Upsala, Universitet.
Vienna, Kaiserliche Königliche Universität.
Wycliffe College, Toronto.
Yale College, New Haven.

Libraries and Corporations.

Birmingham Free Libraries.
Boston Athenæum Library.
Boston Public Library.
Bremen, Stadt-Bibliothek.
Bremerhaven, Stadt-Bibliothek.
British Museum, London.
British Museum (Natural History), London.
Copenhagen, Store kongelige Bibliothek
Edinburgh, Advocates' Library.
Edinburgh, Signet Library.
Glasgow, Mitchell Library.
Guelph Public Library.
London, Guildhall Library,
Melbourne, Public Library, Museums and National Gallery of
    Victoria.
Milwaukee Public Library.
New York, Board of Health.
Royal Botanic Gardens, Kew.
Toronto Public Library.

Societies.

Aarau (Switzerland)—Société Helvétique des Sciences Naturelles.
Aarau (Switzerland)—Aargauische Naturforschende Gesellschaft.
Baltimore—American Economic Association.
Baltimore—American Historical Association.
Berlin—Deutsche Morgenländische Gesellschaft.
Berlin—Geodätisches Institut.
Berlin—Gesellschaft für Erdkunde.
Berlin—Gesellschaft Naturforschender Freunde.

Berlin -Königliche Akademie der Wissenschaften.
Bern—Naturforschende Gesellschaft.
Bonn—Naturhistorischer Verein der Preussischen Rheinlande
 und Westfalens.
Bonn—Niederrheinische Gesellschaft für Natur- und Heilkunde.
Bonn—Verein für Alterthums-Freunde.
Boston—American Society for Psychical Research.
Boston—American Statistical Association.
Boston—Society of Natural History.
Boston—Dante Society.
Boston—Massachusetts Historical Society.
Braunschweig—Allgemeiner deutsche Sprachverein.
Braunschweig—Naturwissenschaftlicher Verein.
Breslau—Landwirthschaftlicher Centralverein für Schlesien.
Breslau—Verein für Schlesische Insectenkunde.
Buffalo—Historical Society.
Buffalo—Society of Natural Science.
Caen—Académie des Sciences, Arts et Belles-Lettres.
Cambridge—Clerk Maxwell Memorial Committee.
Cambridge (U.S.),—American Association for the Advancement
 of Science.
Cambridge (U.S.),—Folk Lore Society.
Cassel—Verein für Naturkunde.
Chapel Hill (U.S.),—Elisha Mitchell Scientific Society.
Chicago—Historical Society.
Christiania—Meteorologiske Institut.
Copenhagen—Carlsberg Fund.
Copenhagen—Society of Sciences.
Danzig—Naturforschende Gesellschaft.
Dewsbury (England),—Yorkshire Archæological and Topogra-
 phical Association.
Douai—Union Géographique du Nord de la France.
Dresden—Naturwissenschaftliche Gesellschaft 'Isis'.
Dresden—Verein für Erdkunde.
Dublin—Royal Academy of Medicine in Ireland.
Dublin—Royal Dublin Society.
Dublin—Royal Irish Academy.

Edinburgh—Royal Scottish Geographical Society.
Edinburgh—Royal Society of Edinburgh.
Edinburgh—Society of Antiquaries of Scotland.
Emden—Naturforschende Gesellschaft.
Frankfurt-am-Main—Freies Deutsches Hochstift.
Frankfurt-a.-M.—Zoologische Gesellschaft.
Frankfurt-an-der-Oder—Naturwissenschaftlicher Verein.
Frauenfeld(Switzerland)—Thurgauischer NaturforschendeVerein
Fribourg (Switzerland)—Société fribourgeoise des Sciences Naturelles.
Giessen—Oberhessische Gesellschaft für Natur- und Heilkunde.
Glasgow—Geological Society.
Glasgow—Institution of Engineers and Shipbuilders in Scotland.
Glasgow—Natural History Society of Glasgow.
Görlitz—Naturforschende Gesellschaft.
Göttingen—Königliche Gesellschaft der Wissenschaften.
Grimsby (Ontario),—Fruit-Growers' Association.
Halifax—Nova Scotian Institute of Natural Sciences.
Halle — Kaiserliche Leopoldinisch-Karolinische Akademie der Naturforscher.
Hamburg—Deutsche Seewarte.
Hamburg—Verein für naturwissenschaftliche Unterhaltung.
Hamburg—Hamburgische wissenschaftliche Anstalten.
Hanau—Wetterauische naturforschende Gesellschaft.
Köln—Görres-Gesellschaft.
Köln—Niederrheinischer Verein für öffentlicheGesundheitspflege.
La Rochelle—Académie des Belles-lettres, Sciences, et Arts.
Leipzig—Königlich-sächsische Gesellschaft der Wissenschaften.
Leipzig—Naturwissenschaftlicher Verein.
Leipzig—Verein für Erdkunde.
Liége—Société Liégeoise de Littérature Wallonne.
London—Ballad Society.
London—Biblical Archæological Society.
London—British Archæological Association.
London—British Association for the Advancement of Science.
London—Chaucer Society.
London—Clinical Society.

London—Early English Text Society.
London—English Dialect Society.
London—Hakluyt Society.
London—Harleian Society.
London—Hibbert Trustees.
London—Howard Association.
London—Imperial Federation League.
London—Institute of Bankers,
London—Institution of Civil Engineers.
London—Mathematical Society.
London—New Shakespere Society.
London—Obstetrical Society.
London—Palestine Exploration Fund Committee.
London—Pathological Society of London.
London—Philological Society.
London—Royal Archæological Institute of GreatBritain and Ireland.
London—Royal Astronomical Society.
London—Royal Colonial Institute.
London—Royal Geographical Society.
London—Royal Institution of Great Britain.
London—Royal Medical and Chirurgical Society.
London—Royal Society.
London—Royal Statistical Society.
London—Society for the Promotion of Hellenic Studies.
London—Society of Antiquaries.
London—Society of Arts.
London—Society of Engineers.
London—Zoological Society of London.
London (Ontario),—Entomological Society of Ontario.
Madison—Wisconson State Historical Society.
Madrid—Real Academia de la Historia.
Magdeburg—Naturwissenschaftlicher Verein.
Manchester—Chetham Society.
Manchester—Manchester Medical Society.
München—Deutsche Gesellschaft für Anthropologie.
München—Geographische Gesellschaft.

Münster—Westfälischer Provinzial-verein für Wissenschaft.
Newcastle-upon-Tyne—Society of Antiquaries of Newcastle-upon-Tyne.
New Haven—American Oriental Society.
New Haven—Connecticut Academy of Arts and Sciences.
New York—American Geographical Society.
New York—American Institute of Mining Engineers.
New York—International Young Men's Christian Association.
New York—New York Academy of Sciences.
New York—New York Historical Society.
New York—New York Microscopical Society.
New York—Society for Political Education.
Niagara Falls (Ontario)—Lundy's Lane Historical Society.
Offenbach-am-Main—Verein für Naturkunde.
Ottawa—Ottawa Field Naturalists' Club.
Ottawa—Royal Society of Canada.
Oxford—Oxford Historical Society.
Paris—Académie des Inscriptions et Belles-lettres, Institut de France
Paris—Société des Ingénieurs Civils.
Paris—Société Mathématique de France.
Paris—Société Zoologique de France.
Philadelphia—Academy of Natural Sciences of Philadelphia.
Philadelphia—American Pharmaceutical Association.
Philadelphia—American Philosophical Society.
Philadelphia—Franklin Institute
Philadelphia—Pennsylvania Historical Society.
Poughkeepsie—Vassar Brothers' Institute.
Quebec—Literary and Historical Society of Quebec.
Rochester (U.S.),—Geological Society of America.
Rome—Reale comitato geologico d'Italia.
Salem—Peabody Academy of Science.
Stettin—Ornithologischer Verein.
St. Louis—Academy of Science of St. Louis.
St. Paul—Minnesota Historical Society.
Stockholm—Kongl. Vitterhets, Historie och Antiquitets Akademien.

Stuttgart—Verein für Vaterländische Naturkunde in Württemberg
Sussex—Sussex Archæological Society.
Sydney (Australia),—Royal Society of New South Wales.
Thorn—Copernicus Verein.
Tokyo—Asiatic Society of Japan.
Tokyo—Seismological Society of Japan.
Topeka—Kansas Academy of Science.
Toronto—Canada Woman's Enfranchisement Association.
Toronto—Canadian Institute.
Toronto—Law Society of Upper Canada.
Toronto—School of Practical Science, Engineering Society.
Washington—American Colonization Society.
Washington—Anthropological Society.
Washington—Biological Society of Washington.
Washington—National Academy of Sciences.
Washington—Philosophical Society of Washington.
Winnipeg—Manitoba Historical & Scientific Society.
Worcester (U.S.),—American Antiquarian Society.
York—Surtees Society.
Zürich—Antiquarische Gesellschaft..
Zwickau,—Verein für Naturkunde.

Publishers and Agents.

Agentur des rauhen Hauses, Hamburg.
Allen, Edward G., London.
American Journal of Science, J. D. & E. S. Dana, New Haven.
American Journal of Morphology, Worcester, U.S.
American Swedenborg Printing and Publishing Society, New York.
American Unitarian Association, Boston.
Appleton & Co., New York.
Asher & Co., London.
Bachem, J P., Köln.
Baedeker, Carl, Leipzig..
Baer & Co., Frankfurt-am-Main.

Bassermann, Fr., München.
Bentley & Sons, London.
Black, A. & C., Edinburgh.
Blackie & Sons, Edinburgh.
Brandstetter, Fr., Leipzig.
British and Foreign Bible Society, London.
British and Foreign Unitarian Association.
Britnell, John, Toronto.
Brockhaus, F. A., Leipzig.
Bruhn, Harald, Braunschweig.
Bryant Co., The J. E., Toronto.
Carswell Company, The, Toronto.
Cassell & Co., London.
Century Company, The, New York.
Chambers, W. & R., Edinburgh.
Church of England Book Society, London.
Clark, T. & T., Edinburgh.
Clive & Co., London.
Conrad's Buchhandlung, Berlin.
Constable, T. & A., Edinburgh.
Copp, Clark Company, The, Toronto.
Costenoble, Hermann, Jena.
Cotta'sche Buchhandlung, Stuttgart.
Daily Graphic, London.
De La Rue & Co., London.
Deutsche Verlagsanstalt, Stuttgart.
Dickenson & Co., Woodstock, Ont.
Douglas, David, Edinburgh.
Dulau & Co., London,
Ernst, A., Dresden.
Eyre & Spottiswoode, London.
Field & Tuer, London.
Fraser, T., Dalbeattie, Scotland.
Friedländer & Sohn, Berlin.
Gärtner's Verlag, Berlin.
Gauthier-Villars et Fils, Paris.
Gilbers'sche Hofbuchhandlung, Dresden.

Ginn & Co., Boston.
Grunow, Fr. Wilh., Leipzig.
Göschen, G. J., Stuttgart.
Guttentag, J., Berlin.
Halberger'sche Buchhandlung.
Harrassowitz, Otto, Leipzig.
Harper & Brothers, New York.
Heath & Co., Boston.
Herder'sche Verlagsbuchhandlung, Freiburg im Breisgau.
Heymann, Carl, Berlin.
Hinstorf'sche Hofbuchhandlung, Wismar.
Hirzel, S., Leipzig.
Holt & Co., New York.
Hölzel, Ed., Wien.
Hunter, Rose & Co., Toronto.
Johnston, W. & A. K., Edinburgh.
Klinksieck, Paul, Paris.
Kochler's Antiquarium, Berlin.
Kohlhammer, W., Stuttgart.
Kröner, Gebrüder, Stuttgart.
Langenscheidt'sche Verlagsbuchhandlung, Berlin.
Laurie, Thomas, London.
Leavenworth Publishing Co., the F. H., Detroit.
Liebmann, Otto, Berlin.
Lippincott Co., the J. B., Philadelphia.
Longmans, Green & Co., London.
Lothrop & Co., Boston.
Low (Sampson), Marston & Co., London.
Macmillan & Bowes, Cambridge.
Macmillan & Co., London.
Meinhold & Söhne, Dresden.
Merriam & Co., Springfield, U.S.
Metzler, J. B., Stuttgart.
Meyer, Carl, Hanover.
Nimmo, John C., London.
Nisbet & Co., London.
Nutt, David, London.

Paetel, Gebrüder, Berlin.
Parker & Co., Oxford.
Paul (Kegan), Trench, Trübner & Co.
Perthes, Justus, Gotha.
Philadelphia Presbyterian Board of Publication.
Pratt, Thos., & Sons.
Publishers' Weekly, New York.
Putnam's Sons, G. P., New York.
Quarterly Journal of Economics, Cambridge, U.S.
Reinwald & Co., Paris.
Roberts Bros., Boston.
Rogers, J. F. K., Melbourne, Australia.
Rolph Smith & Co., Toronto.
Rosenthal's Antiquariat, München.
Routledge & Sons, London.
Rowsell & Hutchison, Toronto.
Schauenburg, Moritz, Lahr.
Scientific Pub. Co., New York.
Scribner's Sons, C., New York.
Smith, R. O., Woodstock, Ont.
Society for the Propagation of the Gospel, London.
Sotheran & Co., London.
Spemann, W., Stuttgart.
Stephens & Sons, London.
Stidstone, C. W., London.
Tauchnitz, Bernhard von, Leipzig.
Teubner, B. G., Leipzig.
Trübner, Karl J., Strassburg.
Virtue, Geo., Toronto.
Virtue, J. S., & Co., London.
Voigt, Bern. Fr., Weimar.
Wagner's Hofbuchhandlung, Braunschweig.
Ward, Lock & Co., London.
Weidmann'sche Buchhandlung, Berlin.
Welter, H., Paris.
Whittaker & Sons, London.
Wiegandt & Grieben, Berlin.

Williams & Norgate, London.
Williamson & Co., Toronto.

Individual Donors.

His Serene Highness the Prince of Monaco.
His Grace the late Duke of Devonshire.
His Grace the Duke of Argyll.
The Most Honourable the Marquis of Ripon.
The Most Honourable the Marquis of Lorne.
The Right Honourable the Earl of Selborne.
The Right Honourable the Earl of Rosebery.
The Right Honourable Lord Tennyson.
The Dowager Lady Vernon.

His Eminence the late Cardinal Manning.
The Right Rev. the Lord Bishop of Southwell.

Abbot, Rev. T. K., Trinity College, Dublin.
Alexander, Prof. W. J. University College, Toronto.
Allan, J. A., Perth, Ont.
Allen, W., Janetville, Ont.
Anschütz, Prof., University of Bonn.
Anthony, Miss Susan B., Rochester, U. S.
Armstrong, Robert Bruce, Edinburgh.
Armstrong, W. R., Owen Sound, Ont.
Ashley, Prof. W. J., University of Toronto.
Ashley, Mrs. W. J., Toronto.
Baensch, W., Dresden.
Baillairgé, C., Quebec.
Bain, James, Jr., Toronto.
Baines, A. W. P., London.
Baldwin, Prof. J. M., University of Toronto.
Baldwin, R. Russell, Toronto.
Ball, G. A., Toronto.
Ball, Sir Robert S., Trinity College, Dublin.
Ball, Rt. Hon. J. T., Dublin.
Bancroft, M. S., Guelph, Ont.

Barwick, Walter, Toronto.
Bell, Prof. A. J., Victoria University, Cobourg, Ont.
Bell, H. T. McKenzie, London.
Binz, Prof. Carl, University of Bonn.
Blackie, Prof. J. S., Edinburgh.
Blackwell, B. H., Oxford.
Blake, Hon. Edward, Toronto.
Bleyt, J., Dresden.
Block, Robert J., London.
Bloomfield, Major J. A., Brighton.
Bourinot, J. G., Ottawa.
Braun, Dr. Adolf, Berlin.
Brebner, J., University of Toronto.
Brinton, Prof. D. G., Media, U.S.
Bronsdon, Geo., Toronto.
Brown, Alex., Toronto.
Brown, Prof. J. Crombie, University of Edinburgh.
Brown, T. Craig, Edinburgh.
Brown-Haddington, Dr.
Browning, Robert Barrett, Venice.
Buchan, Mrs. J. M., Toronto.
Buckham, Geo., New York.
Bulger, ——, Toronto.
Bunbury, Sir E. H., London.
Bürstenbinder, Dr., Braunschweig.
Burton, Hon. Mr. Justice, Toronto.
Campbell, J. H. Mayne, Toronto.
Campbell, Prof. Lewis, University of Aberdeen.
Campbell, Rev. Prof. John, Presbyterian College, Montreal
Carscadden, Thos., Galt, Ont.
Cartwright, Rev. C. E., Kingston, Ont.
Casgrain, L'Abbé, H. R., Université Laval, Quebec.
Cassels, Allan, Toronto.
Chamberlain, A. F., Clark University, Worcester, U.S.
Chapman, Prof, E. J., University of Toronto.
Chase, G. A., Toronto.
Clark, Henry, London.

C

Clementi, Rev. Vincent, Peterborough, Ont.
Cockburn, G. R. R., Toronto.
Connor, J. W., Berlin, Ont.
Cooke, William Henry, London.
Corrado, Prof. S., University of Turin.
Coryton, John, London.
Crosier, Dr. John Beattie, London.
Cumming, Rev. E. C., Portland, Maine.
Dall, Mrs. C. H., Washington.
Davies, Rev John, London.
Davis, Rev. F. W., Blairgowrie, Scotland.
Dawson, Dr. George M., Ottawa.
Dawson, Sir Wm. J., McGill University, Montreal.
De Mazzinghi, Thos. J., Stafford.
Dexter,—, New Haven.
Dickinson, W., Howship, London.
Dietrich, Prof., University of Berlin.
Dittrich, R., Breslau.
Donne, Rev. W., Great Yarmouth, England.
Douglas, W. J., Toronto.
Drummond A. T., Montreal.
Dupont, Paul, Paris.
Edgar, Mrs. J. D., Toronto.
Edmond, E. George, London.
Embree, L. E., Toronto.
Ernst, A., Dresden.
Ernst, Professor, Stuttgart.
Evans, W. Herbert, Forde Abbey, Chard Junction, England.
Ewen, T. E., Belleville.
Eyre, S. Skipton, Leeds.
Falckenberg, Prof. R., University of Erlangen.
Falconbridge, Hon. Mr. Justice, Toronto.
Fawcett, E. H., Ottawa.
Fewkes, H. Walter, Boston.
Flanders, D. J., Boston.
Fletcher, Rev. H., Grasmere, England.
Forbes, Family of the late Bishop, Edinburgh.
Foster, Mrs. W. A., Parry Sound, Ont.

Fotheringham, Rev. T. F., St. John, N. B.
Foxwell, Prof. H. S., St. John's College, Cambridge.
Fraas, Prof. O., Stuttgart.
Fraser, H. B., Toronto.
Fréchette, Louis, Quebec.
Freise, Phillip C., Chicago.
Frey, Prof., Bern, Switzerland.
Frisby, Prof. E., Washington.
Frohschammer, Prof., München.
Fryer, Dr. Alfred C., Bristol.
Garnett, F. B., London.
Garry, Rupert, London.
Gide, C., Paris.
Gilchrist, Rev. J. R., Baltimore, Ont.
Goodwin, Dr. Daniel, New York.
Gorman, Mrs. T., London.
Gould, Jos. E., Uxbridge, Ont.
Graux, Henri, Paris.
Green, W. Henry L., Berlin.
Greenwood, J. G., Eastbourne.
Griffis, Rev. Wm. Elliott, Boston.
De Grouchy, Wm. Lawrence, London.
Hague, George, Montreal.
Hague, John, Toronto.
Hale, Horatio, Clinton, Ont.
Halford-Adcock, Rev. H. H.
Hall, Mrs. Lindsay, Aurora, Ont.
Hall, President G. Stanley, Clark University, Worcester, U. S.
Hamilton, Geo., Middlesbrough, Eng.
Hamilton, Dr. A., Toronto.
Hamilton, J. C., Toronto.
Hanna, Rev. S. C., Uxbridge, Ont.
Hardie, M., Chicago.
Harrison, Reginald, London.
Hartopp, Miss L., Dalby Hall, Melton Mowbray, Leicestershire.
Hauptmann, P., Bonn.
Haverfield, F., Lancing College, England.

Helleberg, C. G., Cincinnati.
Henderson, Miss F. M.
Henshaw, H. W., Washington.
Hertz, Prof. H., University of Bonn.
Heyden, Lawrence, Toronto.
Hiles, Henry, London.
Hill, The Misses Davenport, London.
Hill, Geo. Birkbeck, Oxford.
Hill, Hamnet, Ottawa.
Hill, Mrs. Staveley, London.
Hine, G. A., Toronto.
Hirschfelder, J. M., Toronto.
Hobart, Rev. W. R., Trinity College, Dublin.
Hodgins, Thomas, Toronto.
Hoskin, Alfred, Toronto.
Howes, Prof. G. B., London.
Howland, O. A., Toronto.
Howorth, Henry H., London.
Hoyland, Chas., London.
Humphrey, Dr. G. M., London.
Hüffer, Prof., University of Bonn.
Hutcher, Rev. H.
Hutton, Prof. M., University College, Toronto.
Hyatt, Prof. Alpheus, Boston.
Iles, Geo., New York.
Jacobi, Prof. H.
Jaffray, Robert, Toronto.
Jeffrey, E. C., University of Toronto.
Jessop, Dr. A.
Joest, Herr Wilhelm.
Johnston, J., Ottawa.
Jowett, Prof. Benjamin, Balliol College, Oxford.
Kamphausen, Prof., University of Bonn.
Kelsey, Prof. F. W., Ann Arbor, U.S.
Key, Thomas, London.
Key, The Misses, London.
Keys, David R., University College, Toronto.

King, Joseph, London.
Kingsley, W. L., New Haven.
Koch, G. von, Darmstadt.
Kochs, F., University of Bonn.
Koenig, Dr., University of Bonn.
Kortum, Prof. H., University of Bonn.
Krafft, Prof., University of Bonn.
Lady Undergraduates, University of Toronto.
Laing, A., Edinburgh.
Landauer, Dr. John, Braunschweig.
Langton, H. H., University of Toronto.
Langton, Miss Maria, London.
Laspeyres, Prof. H., University of Bonn.
Laurie, Simon S., Edinburgh.
Ledebur, Prof. A., Freiberg.
Le May, L. P., Quebec.
Le Moine, J. M., Quebec.
Lepsius, Dr. R., Darmstadt.
Leroux, Dr. Jos., Montreal.
Lesslie, Mrs. James, Eglington, Ont.
Lichtenstein, Dr. Ed., Berlin.
Liddell, Rev. Canon Edw., St. Albans.
Lightbody, Andrew, Bellwood, Ont.
Lincke, Herr F., Darmstadt.
Loersch, Prof., University of Bonn.
Loeschke, Prof. G., University of Bonn.
Longstaff, Dr. G. B., London.
Loudon, Prof. James, University of Toronto.
Lumsden, Lieut.-Col., Edinburgh.
Lunge, Prof. G., Zürich.
McCaul, Estate of the late Rev. Dr., first President of University
    College, Toronto.
Macallum, Dr. A. B., University of Toronto.
Maccari, Prof. Andrea, University of Turin.
MacCrae, Mr. D., Guelph, Ont.
McCraney, G. E., Toronto.
McDonald, W., Toronto.
McGee, W. J.

MacIntosh, J. Gray, Brantford, Ont.
McKay, Rev. John, Agincourt, Ont.
MacKendrick, J. N., Galt, Ont.
Mackenzie, J. M., Kingston.
MacKenzie, Estate of the late Walter, Castle Frank, Toronto.
MacLennan, D. B., Cornwall, Ont.
MacNish, Rev. Neil, Cornwall, Ont.
MacNaughton, Rev. Samuel, Preston.
MacQuoid, Wm., St. Albans.
Magee, J. J., Port Hope, Ont.
Malone, Miss Emily, Glasnevin, Ireland.
Manley, F. F., Toronto.
Marriott, Miss, London.
Martineau, J. M., Montreal.
Marx, Prof. Erwin, Darmstadt.
Mason, Miss Amy, Toronto.
Mason, Charles, Hull.
Mason, J. H., Toronto.
Mawr, Mrs. H. B. M., England.
Merritt, J. P., St. Catharines.
Meyer, Dr., Dresden.
Mickle, Dr. W. J., London.
Mik, Prof. J., Vienna.
Miller, Arnoldus, Windsor, N. S.
Miller, Rev. A. E., Hamilton, Ont.
Miln, James, Edinburgh.
Minkowski, Dr., University of Bonn.
Monro, D. B., Oxford.
Montague, Dr., Ottawa.
Montgomery, H., Salt Lake City.
Montt, Pedro, Washington.
Moody, Henry.
Moore, J. Murray, London.
Morgan, Henry J., Ottawa.
Moss, T. H., Toronto.
Moss, Mrs. Thomas, Toronto.
Mott, F. T., London.
Müller, Dr. A., Berlin.

Murphy, J. J., Toronto.
Murrell, Dr. Wm.
Needler, G. H., University College, Toronto.
Neuhauser, Prof. Jos., University of Bonn.
Newman, Rev. Prof. A. H., McMaster University, Toronto.
Nicholson, Prof. H. Alleyne, University of Aberdeen.
Nissen, Prof. H., University of Bonn.
Nodal, J. H., The Grange, Heaton Moore, England.
Oberheimer, Dr. E., München.
Oldright, Dr. W., Toronto.
Oliphant, Mrs. M. O. W., Windsor.
Ormerod, Miss E. A., St. Albans.
Ormiston, David, Whitby, Ont.
Pabst, Reinhold, Delitzsch, Germany.
Parker, Robt. Wm., London.
Parkman, Francis, Boston.
Parsons, Miss Susan, Cheltenham.
Patterson, Rev. Geo., New Glasgow, N. S.
Paton, Rev. Francis L., Princeton, U. S.
Petong, Dr. R., Berlin.
Phillips, Henry, Jr., Philadelphia.
Picard, Charles de, Nancy, France.
Picking, Capt. Henry F., Washington.
Playfair, Rt. Hon. Sir Lyon, London.
Poland, John, London.
Pollock, Sir Frederick, London.
Ponton, W. N., Belleville, Ont.
Pontonié, F., Berlin.
Pottinger, H. A., Worcester College, Oxford.
Pratt, Dr. Henry.
Proudfoot, Hon. Wm., Toronto.
Pyne, J. Kendrick, Manchester.
Raikes, Rt. Hon. H. C., London.
Ramsden, Sir J. W., London.
Ranke, Dr. Johannes, München.
Rauff, H., University of Bonn.
Rein, Prof. J. J., University of Bonn.
Richardson, Dr. J. H., Toronto.

Richarz, Fr., University of Bonn.
Riches, R. H., Toronto.
Roberts, R. D., Cambridge.
Robertson, Prof. G. Croom, University College, London.
Robertson, W. J., St. Catharines, Ont.
Robinson, Sam. S., Orillia, Ont.
Rogers, Walter T., London.
Rohland, Dr., University of Bonn.
Roper, Sydney C. D., Ottawa.
Rosenthal, S., München.
Roth, Jos., München.
Rowson, Rev. Mr.
Rumelin, Ludw., Windischgrätz, Austria.
Rye, Mrs. Amy, Cambridge.
Sachsse, Prof., University of Bonn.
Sacco, Prof. Fredrico, University of Turin.
St. Goar, T., Frankfort am Main.
Salmon, Rev. Provost George, Trinity College, Dublin.
Sanson, Rev. Alex., Toronto.
Saunders, A. P., Ottawa.
Schaaffhausen, Prof., University of Bonn.
Schaarschmidt, Prof., University of Bonn.
Scheffler, Dr. H., Braunschweig.
Scheibler, Prof. C., Berlin.
Schmidt, Dr. Leopold, Marburg.
Schönfeld, Prof. E., University of Bonn.
Scott, Hon. Mrs. Maxwell, Abbotsford, Melrose.
Scott, H. J., Toronto.
Sears, George E , Toronto.
Senkler Estate, per E. J. Reynolds, Brockville, Ont.
Shaw, G. E., Toronto.
Sheldon, E. S., Cambridge, U.S.
Shortt, W. A., New York.
Sidgwick, C. M., Cambridge.
Silver, S. William, London.
Sim, Mr., Woodstock, Ont.
Sime, Mr. & Mrs. James, Chiswick, London.

Sinclair, J. R., Toronto.
Skipton, S. S., London.
Smith, Miss Eliza Carter, London.
Smith, R. O., Woodstock, Ont.
Smith, Rev. Dr. T. Gregory, Malvern.
Smith, William, Ottawa.
Smith, W. J., Brighton.
Smyth, Prof. C. Piazzi, University of Edinburgh.
Snell, H. Saxon, London.
Sommervogel, C., Paris.
Spencer, Rev. E., Tavistock, England.
Squair, John, University College, Toronto.
Stanley, W. Ford, London.
Stephens, Prof. George, University of Copenhagen.
Stokes, Prof. G. T., Trinity College. Dublin.
Stracey, Rev. W. J., London.
Strasburger, Prof. E., University of Bonn.
Streeter, Ed. W., London.
Stricker, R., Berlin.
Strode, E., London.
Struthers, Dr. J., University of Aberdeen.
Stuart, Mrs. G., Okill, Quebec.
Sturn, Dr. R.
Swanwick, Miss Anna, London.
Swinton, A. H., Bedford.
Taché, Louis, Ottawa.
Tarleton, F. A.
Tatham, Rev. Geo. E., East Mosley, England.
Teefy, Rev. J. R., St. Michael's College, Toronto.
Temple, Sir Richard, London.
Tennant, Gen., London.
Thom, A. Bissett, London.
Thom, Mrs. D., Liverpool.
Thom, J. H., Toronto.
Todd, George, London.
Tozer, Ephraim, Toronto.
Uschner, Dr. Oppeln, Germany.
Usener, Prof. H., University of Bonn.

Valle, Prof. Guido, University of Turin.
VanderSmissen, W. H., University College, Toronto.
Vicars, Mrs., Toronto.
Wagner, Fried., Brunswick.
Waterhouse, S., Washington University.
Weiss, Georg, Heidelberg.
Wells, H., Wadham College, Oxford.
Wendt, Ernst Emil, London.
Whiting, Hon. J. W.
Wicksteed, G. W., Ottawa.
Wilkie, D. R., Toronto.
Willeman, Prof. L. von, Darmstadt.
Williams, George E., Kingston, Ont.
Williamson, Prof. B., University of Dublin.
Williamson, Mrs., Toronto.
Williamson, T. G.
Willman, Wm.
Wilson, Sir Daniel, University of Toronto.
Wilton, Chas., St. Alban's.
Winchell, N. H.
Winkler, Dr. Clemens, Frieberg.
Wishart, Dr. D. J. Gibb, Toronto.
Wissler, Henry, Elora, Ont.
Withrow, Rev. W. H., Toronto.
Woodhouse, J. J., Toronto.
Woods, Samuel, London, Ont.
Wright, A. G., Malvern.
Wright, A. W., Galt, Ont.
Wrong, Rev. G. M., Wycliffe College, Toronto.
Wülker, Prof. Richard Paul, University of Leipzig.
Young, C. A., Princeton, U. S.
Young, Hon. James, Galt, Ont.
Zais, Ernst, Munich.
Zeller, Prof. E., University of Berlin.

The above list embodies a record of the Benefactors to whose generous sympathy the University is so largely indebted for the restoration of its Library. A detailed record of their gifts would involve the printing of a Library Catalogue of upwards of 30,000 volumes.

SUBSCRIPTIONS.

LIBRARY BUILDING.

Alexander, D. W., Toronto..... ....$	100	00
Bank of Commerce, Toronto......................	1,000	00
Barbour, Dr. Hugh, Edinburgh...................	2,422	22
Beatty, W. H., Toronto..........................	1,000	00
Bell, Bigg & Cowan..............................	100	00
Buntin, Reid & Co., Toronto.....................	100	00
Caldecott, Burton & Co., Toronto	100	00
Cawthra, the late Joseph, formerly of Toronto......	500	00
Christie, W., Toronto............................	5,000	00
Copp Clark Co., The, Toronto.	100	00
Cox, Geo. A., Toronto	5,000	00
Cumberland, Miss, Toronto.......................	3	00
Davidson & Hay, Toronto........................	1,012	50
Dowsley, Rev. A................................	4	40
Goldsmith Company, London......................	241	67
Gooderham, George, Toronto.....................	10,000	00
Gooderham, W. J., Toronto.......................	1,000	00
Hamilton, W. B................................	250	00
Hammond, H. C., Toronto.................... ..	1,000	00
Hoskin, Dr. John, Toronto.......................	1,000	00
Jamieson, P., Toronto......................	500	00
Keith, John, Toronto.............	200	00
Kilgour Bros., Toronto...........................	500	00
McConnell, M., Toronto.........................	100	00
McGaw & Winnett, Toronto........	250	00
Mathews. W. D., Toronto..................	1,000	00
Milburn, T., Toronto.............................	200	00

Mulock, W., Toronto..	$ 5,000 00
Nelson, H. W., Toronto..	100 00
Osler, E. B., Toronto............................	10,000 00
Pugsley, John, Toronto..............................	200 00
Quebec, Grant from Province of.........	10,000 00
Rogers, Elias & Co., Toronto......................	100 00
Scott, James, Toronto.............................	500 00
Smart, Mrs. Emily, Cobourg	500 CO
Smith, Dr. Andrew, Toronto.......................	500 00
Smith, Dr. Larratt W., Toronto....................	500 00
Sweny, Col., Toronto..............................	500 00
Warwick & Sons, Toronto	100 00
Wyld, Grasett & Darling, Toronto.................	200 00

LIBRARY RESTORATION FUND (Books).

Acheson, Dr. George, Toronto.....	$ 50 00
Aikenhead & Crombie, Toronto..............	25 00
Aikins, Dr. H. Wilberforce, Toronto.........	100 00
Aikins, B. M., Toronto	25 00
Alexander, A....	5 00
Alexander, Prof. W. J., Toronto.....	250 00
Allan, A. A., Toronto..................	100 00
Allan, H. & H. A., Montreal....	200 00
Allen, W. McC., Millbrook..	50 00
Angus, R. B.....................	100 00
Annis, J. W., St. Thomas...........	10 00
Anonymous.....	20 00
Armstrong, T. C. L., Toronto......	100 00
Ashley, Prof. W. J., Toronto........ ..	100 00
Austin, B. F., St. Thomas...................	20 00
Baker, Prof. Alfred, Toronto.................. ..	250 00
Bain, James, Jr., Toronto........................	25 00

Baldwin, Rev. J. Macqueen, Japan.................$	150 00
Baldwin, Prof J. Mark, Toronto....................	100 00
Baldwin, Robt., Toronto.................	100 00
Baldwin, W. W., Toronto........................	100 00
Ballard, W. H., Hamilton........................	100 00
Balmer, Miss E. M., Strathroy....................	25 00
Banks, G. W., Toronto...	25 00
Barber & Ellis Co., Toronto.....................	100 00
Barker, P. M., Regina, N.W.T....................	50 00
Barrie Collegiate Institute......................	100 00
Barton, Dr. S. G. T., Toronto...................	25 00
Bascom, Dr. Jos., Uxbridge......................	25 00
Beardmore & Co., Toronto.	300 00
Beck, H. T., Toronto...........................	100 00
Bell, Prof. A. J., Cobourg.......................	40 00
Bell Telephone Co., Montreal.....	100 00
Bell, W. N., Strathroy..........................	5 00
Bertram, John, Toronto.........................	50 00
Bettridge, Dr. Wm., Strathroy	10 00
Bigelow, N. Gordon, Toronto.....................	100 00
Biggar, C. R. W., Toronto.......................	1,000 00
Bilton Bros., Toronto...	25 00
Blackstock, G. T., Toronto.......................	50 00
Blackstock, Mrs. G. T., Toronto..................	200 00
Blackstock, Joseph, Toronto......................	25 00
Blaikie, J. L., Toronto..........................	100 00
Blake, Lash & Cassels, Toronto..	1,000 00
Blue, A., Toronto..............................	100 00
Bonis, H., Toronto.............................	10 00
Boulton, C. R., Toronto........	50 00
Bowman, L. & A., Lindsay......................	50 00
Boyd, Hon. Chancellor, Toronto..................	25 00
Boys, Judge, Barrie..	25 00
Bradley, W. J., Sault Ste. Marie.................	100 00
Brebner, James, Toronto........................	25 00
Brennan, H. S., Hamilton.......	25 00
Brierley, J. S., St. Thomas.....................	10 00

Brown Bros., Toronto ....$	250 00
Brown, J. Gordon, Toronto	25 00
Bryce, Dr. Peter H., Toronto......................	250 00
Buchan, Dr. H. E., Toronto......................	100 00
Buckham, G., New York	25 00
Bull, B. E., Toronto............................	100 00
Burnham, Dr. G. H., Toronto...................	50 00
Burnham, J. H., Peterboro'......................	50 00
Burns, John....................................	50 00
Burritt, W. E., Toronto.........................	10 00
Burritt, W. C...................................	15 00
Burrows, J. C., Toronto.........................	50 00
Burt, Dr. F., Norwalk, Ohio.....................	10 00
Burton, G. F., Toronto.........................	100 00
Cameron, D. O., Toronto..	100 00
Cameron, E. R., London........................	100 00
Cameron, Prof. J. C............................	5 00
Cameron, L. H.................................	100 00
Campbell, Mrs. A. F., Toronto	100 00
Campbell, A. H., Jr., Toronto................... ..	250 00
Campbell, J. S., St. Catharines....................	25 00
Campbell, Rev. Prof. John, Montreal	100 00
Cane, G. F., Toronto	25 00
Canniff, H. T , Toronto	50 00
Carpenter, Henry, Hamilton..	25 00
Carpmael, Charles, Toronto.......................	150 00
Carruthers, A., Toronto.........................	30 00
Carscadden, T., Galt...........................	30 00
Carveth, Dr. Geo. H., Toronto...................	25 00
Case, G. A....................................	50 00
Cassels, R. S., Toronto.........................	100 00
Catto & Co., John, Toronto......................	250 00
Cave, G. F....................................	25 00
Caven, Rev. Principal, Toronto	100 00
Chamberlain, A. F., Worcester, U.S................	25 00
Chambers, Dr. G., Toronto......................	50 00
Chapman, Prof. E. J., Toronto	250 00

Charles, Miss Henrietta ....$	25 00
Chase, G. A., Toronto............................	50 00
Chewett, Dr. W. C., Toronto.......	200 00
Chisholm, James, Hamilton	50 00
Chisholm, W. C., Toronto..	100 00
Clarkson, E. R. C., Toronto......................	100 00
Clayton, Miss A. H. R., Ridgetown...	25 00
Clement, W. H. P., Toronto...	1,000 00
Coatsworth, Emerson, Toronto.....................	200 00
Cockshutt, C. & Co..........	100 00
Cody, H. J., St. Catharines.......................	10 00
Collier, H. H., St. Catharines.............	50 00
Congdon, Fred. T., Halifax	50 00
Cook, W., Toronto........	200 00
Cosby, A. M., Toronto.	500 00
Courtice, A. C., Port Perry	15 00
Covernton, Dr. T. S., Toronto....................	50 00
Coyne, J. H., St. Thomas	100 00
Craig, J. A., Madison, Wis....	25 00
Craig, Rev. John...... ....,......	5 00
Craik, Rev. Prof................................	25 00
Crawford, J. T., Hamilton	25 00
Crawford, J., Toronto........................	20 00
Crawford, W. G., Toronto........................	50 00
Creelman, A. R., Toronto	100 00
Creelman, Geo. C...........................	10 00
Crombie, Marcellus, Toronto......................	250 00
Cronyn & Betts, London	150 00
Crooks, A. D., Toronto.......................	50 00
Cumberland, Miss F., Toronto.....................	2 00
Cumberland, Wilmot, Toronto	5 00
Cumming, Montgomery, Washington................	100 00
Curzon, Miss E. M., Toronto....	25 00
Cuthbert, James, Ingersoll.......................	100 00
Dale, William, Toronto	150 00
Davidson, L. B., Toronto..................	50 00
Davison, Dr. J. L., Toronto...........	50 00

Davis, E. P., Calgary, N. W. T.. ... .$	100 00
Dayfoot, P. K., Strathroy.........................	10 00
Deguerre, A., Strathroy	25 00
Delamere, T. D., Toronto..................	200 00
DeLury, A. T., Toronto............................	25 60
Dewart, H. H. & Irving, W. H., Toronto...........	100 00
Dick, D. B., Toronto.............................	500 00
Dickson, George, Toronto.......................	50 00
Dickson, J. E., Newmarket.......................	10 00
Doherty. W. B., St. Thomas.....................	50 00
Donald, R. C., Toronto..........................	30 00
Douglas, W. A., Toronto.........................	20 00
Drake, F. A., Toronto	50 00
Duff, John A., Clover Hill	25 00
Duggan, E. H., Toronto....	100 00
Dunn, H. L., Toronto	100 00
Dwight, H. P., Toronto.	100 00
Eakins, J. E., Belleville	25 00
Eakins, W. G., Toronto...........................	100 00
Eastman, S. H., Oshawa.........................	25 00
Eastwood, Miss I. G.,Whitby.....................	10 00
Eby, Blain & Co., Toronto........................	100 00
Eccles, F. R.........	100 00
Edwards, E. B., Peterboro'..................	100 00
Elliott, A., Toronto.......	50 00
Elliott, T. E., Ingersoll.....	25 00
Ellis, Dr. W. H., Toronto........................	250 00
Embree, L. E., Toronto.........................	100 00
Ewen, T. E., Belleville	10 00
Fair, Caroline, Toronto..........................	25 00
Fairclough, H. R., Toronto	100 00
Falconbridge, Hon. Mr. Justice. Toronto...........	300 00
Fee, John, Guelph.............................	10 00
Ferguson, G. H., Kemptville......................	5 00
Ferguson, Dr. John, Toronto.....................	100 00
Field, Dr. Byron, Toronto........................	20 00
Field, G. W. Guelph.............................	50 00

Fife, J. A., Peterboro'......................................$	25 00
Fisken, J. Kerr, Toronto................................	500 00
Fletcher, B	10 00
Forbes, Robert................................	50 00
Fotheringham, Dr. J. T., Toronto............	25 00
Fraser, Colin, Toronto............................	25 00
Fraser, G. A. H., Deer Lodge, Montana..........	50 00
Fraser, W. H., Toronto..........................	100 00
"Friend," Legislative Assembly, Toronto............	1 00
Galbraith, D. E., St. Thomas....................	10 00
Galbraith, Prof. J., Toronto................	150 00
Galbraith, Mr...........................	4 78
Galt, A. C., Toronto........................	50 00
Gardiner, Miss E., Belleville.....................	25 00
Garvin, J. W., Woodstock	25 00
Gibbard, Alex. H., Brantford.................	100 00
Gibson, G., Toronto........................	50 00
Gibson, Hon. J. M., Hamilton	250 00
Gibson, Rev. J. M.......................	24 33
Gill, James, Toronto..........................	25 00
Glass, C. T., London........................	25 00
Glenn, James, Toronto	20 00
Globe Correspondent	1 00
Goldie, John..............................	25 00
Gould, Joseph E., Uxbridge.................	10 00
Gourlay, R., Oshawa........................	50 00
Grant, Wilbur, Toronto....................	50 00
Gray, R. A., London........................	25 00
Green, George M., Halifax.	50 00
Green, Mrs., Toronto......................	5 00
Greer, George M., Halifax...................	50 00
Gregg, Mrs. J...........................	5 00
Gregory, E. Arnold..	5 00
Greig, Major George, Toronto	100 00
Grier, Miss R. J. E., Toronto..............	100 00
Grierson, J. F., Oshawa...................	50 00
Günther, Ernest, Toronto..................	50 00

Gwynne, W. D., Toronto...........................$ 100 00
Hague, Rev. Dyson, Halifax........................ 25 00
Hamilton, Rev. H. J., Toronto.................... 100 00
Hanna, Rev. W. G., Uxbridge 15 00
Harcourt, George, Charlottetown... .... 10 00
Hare, Rev. J. J., Whitby........ .... 20 00
Hardy, E. A., Lindsay.......... .... 75 00
Harris, Rev. Dean.. .... 5 00
Harvey, Horace, Toronto 100 00
Hatton, J. Cassie, Montreal...................... 25 00
Hemingway, Mr.. .... 10 21
Henderson, A., Oshawa........................... 25 00
Henderson, J., St. Catharines 50 00
Hill, Rev. Arundel C., St. Thomas................. 100 00
Hill, Miss Davenport, London..................... 24 30
Hill, E. L., Woodstock............. .... 50 00
Hodgson, J. E., Toronto.......................... 50 00
Hodgins, Rev. Fred. B., St. Catharines............. 50 00
Hogarth, E. B., Woodstock 10 00
Hoig, Dr., Oshawa 25 00
Holmes, G. W., Toronto......................... 100 00
Hope, R. A............................... 5 00
Horton, Albert, Toronto 25 00
Hoskin, Dr. John, Toronto..................... 100 00
Houston, William, Toronto....................... 100 00
Howland, O. A., Toronto 250 00
Hughes, James L., Toronto....................... 50 00
Hull, Daniel, Toronto............................. 25 00
Hull, J. F., Toronto.............................. 10 00
Hunt, E. Lawrence, Guelph............. .... 50 00
Hunter, A. F., Barrie...... .... 25 00
Hunter, D. H., Woodstock........................ 25 00
Hunter, J. M., Barrie. 25 00
Huston, Principal W. H., Woodstock............... 50 00
Hutton, Prof. Maurice, Toronto 150 00
James, C. C., Guelph........................ .... 10 00
Janes, S. H., Toronto............................. 500 00

Jarvis, Miss Julia..........................$	5 00
Jeffrey, E. C., Toronto......................	100 00
Jeffries, J., Peterboro'......................	25 00
Johnson, George, Ottawa	100 00
Johnston, R. L., Toronto....................	25 00
Jones, Miss.............	25 00
Kay, John, Son & Co., Toronto...............	500 00
Keefer, Frank H., Port Arthur...............	100 00
Kennedy, Dr. George, Toronto................	100 00
Kent, H., Toronto	10 00
Kerr, C. S., Woodstock	15 00
Kerr, Rev. F. W., Toronto	5 00
Kerr, John R., Barrie......................	15 00
Kerr, M.............................	100 00
Kerr, Macdonald, Davidson & Paterson, Toronto	800 00
Kerr, W. H. C., Toronto....................	400 00
Keys, D. R., Toronto.......................	100 00
King, Joseph J.	9 68
Kingston, F. W	50 00
Knox, William...........................	10 00
Lady, per T. D. Delamere.	10 00
Lamport, W. A., Toronto....................	10 00
Langton, H. H., Toronto....................	250 00
Langton, T., Toronto.......................	100 00
Larkin, P., St. Catharines..................	50 00
Lawrence, A. G. F., Toronto................	25 00
Lee, Lyman, Hamilton......................	50 00
Lee, Walter S., Toronto....................	100 00
Lennox, Haughton, Barrie...................	25 00
Lennox, T. H., Woodstock..................	25 00
Little, J. G., Ridgetown...................	50 00
Little, R. A., London.....................	25 00
Long, J. H., Camden, N.Y..................	50 00
Long, Mr	4 87
Loudon, Prof. J., Toronto.................$	250 00
Loudon, W. J., Toronto....................	100 00
Lount, Samuel, Barrie	25 00

Lyman, Bros. & Co., Toronto	$ 50	00
Macallum, Dr. A. B., Toronto	100	00
McAndrew, J. A., Toronto	100	00
Macbeth, T., London	100	00
McCabe, Wm., Toronto	200	00
McCaul, C. C., Lethbridge, N. W.T	100	00
McClive, W. H., St. Catharines	50	00
McConnell, F. W., Toronto	5	00
McCrae, D., Guelph	100	00
McCurdy, Prof. J. F., Toronto	100	00
Macdonald, A. A., Toronto	5	00
Macdonald, G. S., Montreal	50	00
Macdonald, W	2	00
Macdonell, A. McLean, Toronto	50	00
Macdonell, Rev. D. J., Toronto	100	00
McEachren, Prof. D	25	00
McEachren, Neil, Toronto	50	00
McEachren, P., Toronto	50	00
McFarlane, Dr. L., Toronto	100	00
McGeary, J. H., St. Thomas	100	00
McGowan, J., Toronto	40	00
McGuire, W. J. & Co., Toronto	100	00
McHarrie, R. C., Toronto	10	00
McIntyre, F. J., Toronto	50	00
McKay, A. C., Toronto	30	00
McKay, John A., Toronto	$ 25	00
McKay, Rev. W. A., Woodstock	25	00
McKendrick, J. N., Galt	25	00
Mackenzie, J. J., Toronto	40	25
McKenzie, Dr. K., St. Thomas	10	00
McKenzie, John J., Toronto	25	00
McKenzie, Dr. T., Toronto	100	00
McKeown, John, St. Catharines	50	00
Mackinnon, Dr. A., Guelph	100	00
McLaren, Prof., Toronto	25	00
McLarty, Dr. D., St. Thomas	10	00
Maclean, C. G., Toronto	250	00

McMaster & Co., Toronto	500	00
MacMurchy, Angus, Toronto	100	00
MacMurchy, Archibald, Toronto	100	00
MacMurchy, Helen, Toronto	25	00
McPherson, R U., Toronto	100	00
MacRae, N., Toronto	5	00
Manley, F. F., Toronto	100	00
Marsh, A. H., Toronto	200	00
Martland, John, Toronto	25	00
Mason, J. Herbert, Toronto	100	00
Matchett, R. J., Lindsay	25	00
Meredith, W. R., Toronto	100	00
Merritt, W. H., Toronto	15	00
Meyer, H. W. C., Wingham	100	00
Michie, George S., Toronto	50	00
Mickle, H. W., Toronto	100	00
Milden, A. W., Barrie	25	00
Millar, Charles, Toronto	200	00
Millar, John, St. Thomas	50	00
Miller, Rev. J. O., St. Catharines	50	00
Miller, James, Toronto	30	00
Miller, W. N., Toronto	40	00
Mills, James, Guelph	50	00
Mills, Prof. Wesley, Montreal	5	00
Milner, W. S., Toronto	100	00
Mitchell, Rev. A. E., Almonte	10	00
Molyneaux, G.	10	22
Montgomery, J. D., Toronto	50	00
Montreal Gazette, Montreal	20	00
Moore, W. H., Peterboro'	50	00
Morgan, H. A., Baton Rouge, Ia	10	00
Morgan, J. C., Barrie	25	00
Mortimer, Edward, Toronto	20	00
Morton, Dr. E. D., Barrie	25	00
Moss, Charles, Toronto	500	00
Moss, Hoyles & Aylesworth, and Moss, Barwick & Franks, Toronto	1000	00

Mowat, Mr. Sheriff, Toronto	$ 500	00
Mulvey, Thomas, Toronto	40	00
Murray, W. A., & Co., Toronto	500	00
Neil, Rev. John, Toronto	30	00
Nesbitt, Dr. W. B., Toronto	100	00
Northrop & Lyman, Toronto	1000	00
O'Brien, A. H., Toronto	50	00
O'Flynn, F. E., Belleville	100	00
Oldwright, Dr. Wm., Toronto	100	00
Osler, B. B., Toronto	500	00
O'Sullivan, Dr. D. A., Toronto	100	00
Page, J. A., Toronto	100	00
Park, H. G., Uxbridge	5	00
Parkdale Collegiate Institute	130	00
Parlane, W. A	20	0₀
Paterson, B. Eton, Sackville, N.B	10	00
Perth Literary Institute.	15	00
Peters, Dr. George A., Toronto	25	00
Philip, James H., Barrie	25	00
Pike, Prof. W. H., Toronto	258	33
Ponton, W. N., Belleville	25	00
Ponton, J. Hayes, Guelph	50	00
Pope, Hon. C. H., Toronto, proceeds of Lecture on Shakespeare	123	50
Proudfoot, W. A., London	25	00
Radenhurst, G. A., Barrie	25	00
Radford, Dr. J. H., Galt	25	00
Rae, Dr. Francis, Oshawa	25	00
Raines, F. N., Uxbridge	25	00
Rathbun, E. W., Deseronto	100	00
Raynor, T., Rose Hall	5	00
Redpath, Peter	97	22
Reesor, H. A., Toronto	100	00
Reeve, Dr. R. A., Toronto	100	00
Reid, Rev. H. E. A. Toronto	10	00
Reynolds, A., Strathroy	5	00
Richardson, George H., Chatham	50	00

Riddell, G. I., Parkdale	$ 12	50
Rivington, Messrs., London	50	00
Roaf, Wm., Toronto	100	00
Robertson, Charles, Hamilton	50	00
Robertson, Miss Madge, Toronto	25	00
Robertson, Dr. S. E., Newark, N.J	200	00
Robertson, W. J., St. Catharines	25	00
Robinson, Christopher, Toronto	100	00
Robinson, George E. H., Toronto	50	00
Robinson, Samuel, Orillia	10	00
Robson, Miss Jessie H., Walkerton	25	00
Rolph, Smith & Co., Toronto	25	00
Roseburgh, Mr.	4	87
Ross, R., Peterboro'	25	00
Ross, Dr. W. A.	5	00
Rowsell & Hutchison, Toronto	250	00
Ryerson, C. E., Toronto	50	00
Rykert, E. G., St. Catharines	20	00
Saunders, B.	25	00
Scott, H. J., Toronto	1000	00
Scott, J. J.	100	00
Scott, J. Mc P., Toronto	25	00
Scott, W. D., Peterboro'	100	00
Seath, John, Toronto	50	00
Seymour, Fred F., Madoc	100	00
Shaw, N., Toronto	25	00
Shepherd, W. G., St. Thomas	50	00
Shortt, W. A., New York	50	00
Simpson, T. Walker, Toronto	50	00
Sinclair, John R., Toronto	25	00
Small, J. T., Toronto	100	00
Smith, Sir Donald, Montreal	1000	00
Smith, G. A., Toronto	30	00
Smith, George, Woodstock	25	00
Smith, George H., Toronto	50	00
Smith, J. F. Berkeley, Toronto	100	00
Smith, L. H., Strathroy	10	00

Smoke, S. C., Toronto	$ 100	00
Somers, F., Toronto	25	00
Somerville, T. C., London, Ont	25	00
Sparling, J. A., Strathroy	25	00
Spence, Miss Nellie, Toronto	30	00
Spencer, Dr. B., Toronto	50	00
Spotton, H. B., Toronto	25	00
Spotton, W. H. B., Toronto	10	00
Sproule, R. K., Toronto	100	00
Squair, J., Toronto	100	00
Standing, T. W., Burford	5	00
Stayner, F. Sutherland, Toronto	50	00
Steen, Frederick J., St. Catharines	10	00
Stevenson, A., Peterboro'	100	00
Stevenson, A., Toronto	10	00
Stewart, James	5	00
Stewart, Louis B., Toronto	50	00
Stewart, F. J	100	00
Stewart, Miss E. M., Aylmer	25	00
Stirton, D., Guelph	50	00
Strathroy Collegiate Institute	25	00
Stratton, A. W., Hamilton	50	00
Stuart, C. A., Brooklyn, N.Y	03	00
Swan Bros., Toronto	10	00
Sykes, Fred H., Toronto	30	00
Tabey, C. W	10	00
Tait, D. M., St. Thomas	10	00
Taylor Bros., Toronto	300	00
Thomas, Miss J., Toronto	25	00
Thomas, Miss L., Toronto	15	00
Thompson, Mrs. Agnes, Toronto	25	00
Thompson, A. Stewart, Strathroy	10	00
Thompson, C. E., Toronto	30	00
Thompson, R. A., Hamilton	50	00
Thompson, Thomas, & Son, Toronto	100	00
Thomson, Rev. R. Y., Toronto	60	00
Tobey, C. W., Collingwood	10	00

Toronto Collegiate Institute, Toronto............ .... $	42 00
Toronto Orchestral Society, proceeds of two concerts..	114 56
Tracy, F., Toronto................................	10 00
Tytler W., Guelph	100 00
Thorburn, Dr. I., Toronto........................	100 00
Urquhart, D., Toronto...................	100 00
Vandersmissen, W. H., Toronto	100 00
Veals, Miss, Toronto............................	5 00
Vogt, A. S., Toronto..............................	20 00
Walker, B. E., Toronto...........................	1000 00
Walker, W. F., Hamilton.....................	100 00
Wallace, Rev. Prof., Cobourg.........	100 00
Wallace, M. J..	1 00
Wallace, Edward Wilson, Cobourg.................	3 00
Wallace, Rev. W. G., Toronto.......	20 00
Warner, R. I., St. Thomas..............	10 00
Watt, James, Guelph.............	50 00
Wedd, William, Toronto.........................	25 00
Weir, A., Peterboro'.....	100 00
Weld, Dr. O., London.....	25 00
Wetherell, J. E., Strathroy....................	50 00
White, Richard, Montreal............	
Wickett, W. L., St. Thomas	10 00
Wightman, John R., Grinnell, Ia..............	60 00
Wilkins, Dr. George, Montreal................	5 00
Williams, Green, Rome & Co., Toronto	100 00
Willmott, Dr. J. B., Toronto	25 00
Wilson, Sir Daniel, Toronto....................... .	250 00
Wishart, Dr. D. J. G., Toronto....................	50 00
Wismer, J. A., Toronto...........................	30 00
Witton, H. B., Sr., Hamilton.....................	15 00
Witton, H. B., Jr., Hamilton.....................	50 00
Wolverton, N., Woodstock.	50 00
Wood, S. G., Toronto.................	50 00
Wood, Mrs	24 33
Woods, S., London	100 00
Wright, A. W., Galt........................... ..	40 00

Wright, Dr. A. H., Toronto.........................$ 100 00
Wright, George S., Belleville........................   50 00
Wright, Prof. R. Ramsay, Toronto.................. 250 00
Yale, H., St. Catharines..... ....   25 00
Young, A. H., Toronto.... ....   25 00
Young, Sir F 24 35
Zavitz, C. A., Guelph.... ....   10 00

www.ingramcontent.com/pod-product-compliance
Lightning Source LLC
Chambersburg PA
CBHW022031080426
42733CB00007B/806